THE 100 HATS OF THE CAT IN THE HAT

I'm the Cat in the Hat
and today is the best—
I am going to visit
your school as a guest!

The Cat in the Hat's Learning Library®
introduces beginning readers to basic non-
fiction. If your child can read these lines,
then he or she can begin to understand the
fascinating world in which we live.

Learn to read. Read to learn.

This book comes from the home of

THE CAT IN THE HAT
RANDOM HOUSE

For a list of books in **The Cat in the Hat's**
Learning Library, *see the back endpaper.*

To my friends Sheila Murphy Adams and Stacey Daly, two of the millions of caring, dedicated teachers who help our children learn every day.
—T.R.

The editors would like to thank
BARBARA KIEFER, Ph.D.,
Charlotte S. Huck Professor of Children's Literature,
The Ohio State University, and
NICOLE FLETCHER, Ph.D.,
Teachers College, Columbia University,
for their assistance in the preparation of this book.

Visit us on the Web!
Seussville.com
rhcbooks.com

Educators and librarians, for a variety of teaching tools, visit us at RHTeachersLibrarians.com

Library of Congress Cataloging-in-Publication Data is available upon request.
ISBN 978-0-525-57995-3 (trade) — ISBN 978-0-525-57996-0 (lib. bdg.)

Printed in the United States of America

10 9 8 7 6 5 4 3 2 1

First Edition

THE 100 HATS OF THE CAT IN THE HAT

by Tish Rabe

illustrated by Aristides Ruiz and Joe Mathieu

The Cat in the Hat's Learning Library®

Random House 🏠 New York

I'm the Cat in the Hat,
and today is the best—
I am going to visit
your school as a guest!

You've been counting for months,
and I'm happy to say
the 100th day of
your school year is TODAY!

Get ready to count,

multiply, and divide.

We don't want to be late,

so jump in and let's ride!

On this 100th day
I brought 100 hats.
We can use them when we start
to add and subtract.

But first let's start counting.
I'll show you a chart.
It's a hundreds chart,
and I know it by heart.

Count from 1 to 100.
Let's give it a try.
This chart will help us,
and soon you'll see why.

Now let's try skip counting.

I could do it all day!

We can count to 100

in a much faster way.

We can skip count by fives . . .

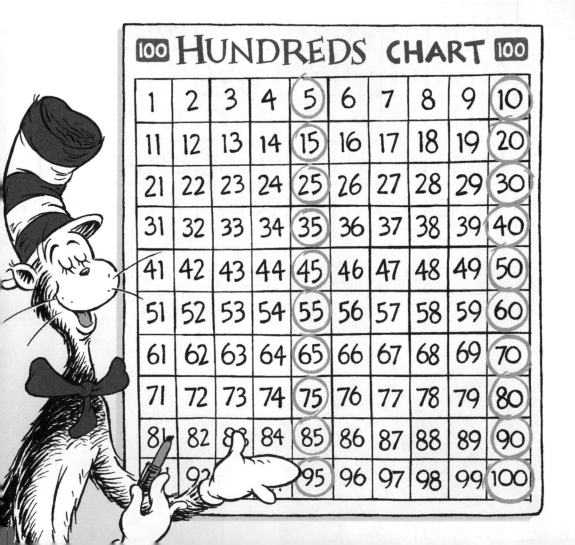

100 HUNDREDS CHART 100

1	2	3	4	5	6	7	8	9	10
11	12	13	14	15	16	17	18	19	20
21	22	23	24	25	26	27	28	29	30
31	32	33	34	35	36	37	38	39	40
41	42	43	44	45	46	47	48	49	50
51	52	53	54	55	56	57	58	59	60
61	62	63	64	65	66	67	68	69	70
71	72	73	74	75	76	77	78	79	80
81	82	83	84	85	86	87	88	89	90
91	92	93	94	95	96	97	98	99	100

. . . or skip count by tens.

Let's count to 100—

then do it again!

100	HUNDREDS CHART	100

1	2	3	4	5	6	7	8	9	(10)
11	12	13	14	15	16	17	18	19	(20)
21	22	23	24	25	26	27	28	29	(30)
31	32	33	34	35	36	37	38	39	(40)
41	42	43	44	45	46	47	48	49	(50)
51	52	53	54	55	56	57	58	59	(60)
61	62	63	64	65	66	67	68	69	(70)
71	72	73				77	78	79	(80)
81	82	83				87	88	89	(90)
						97	98	99	(100)

Another way I count
(this is one of my tricks)
is to get a big pile
of Popsicle sticks!

I count sticks by ones
until I have 10.
Then I bundle 10 sticks
and start counting again.

When I have 10 bundles
it's easy to see
I have 100 sticks—
you can count them with me.

Now let's add some hats.
When I'm adding I choose
to make ten frames because
they are easy to use.

I put 10 hats in each frame.
The ten frames make it clear.
10 hats in ten frames—
there are 100 hats here.

$$10 + 10 + 10 + 10 + 10$$
$$+ 10 + 10 + 10 + 10 + 10 = 100$$

10 TEN Frames

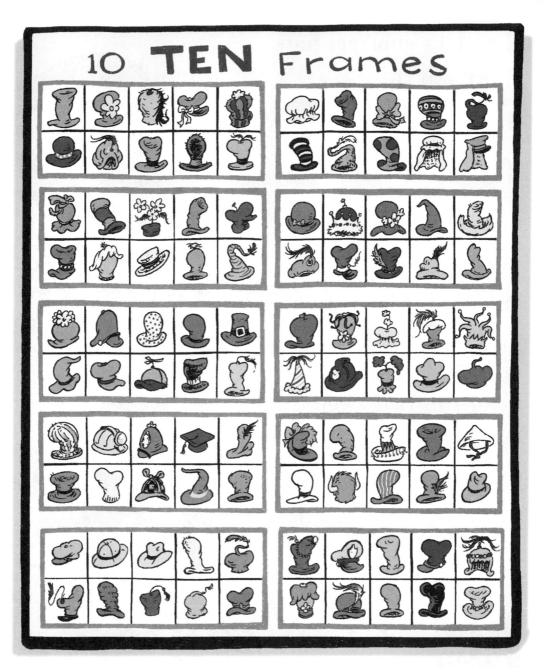

Here is a fact that
I learned from Thing One—
when you add numbers, the total
is known as the sum.

Next let's subtract hats,
and I will show you
that ten frames make subtraction
easy to do.

I have ten frames with 10 hats,
as you may recall,
but what if I decide
I do not need them all?

I can subtract 2 ten frames.
(2 ten frames is 20.)
I have 80 hats left,
and for me, that is plenty!

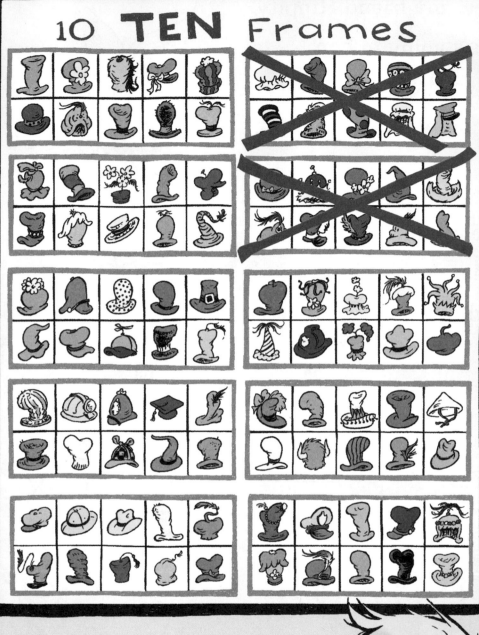

100-20=80

Meet my friend Hippity!
She's going to hop
down the number line.
Where will Hippity stop?

Hippity hops so that
she can show you
the sum of 58
and 42.

Hippity

58   68   78

She starts at 58,

then hops over 10 logs,

10 flower pots,

10 friendly frogs,

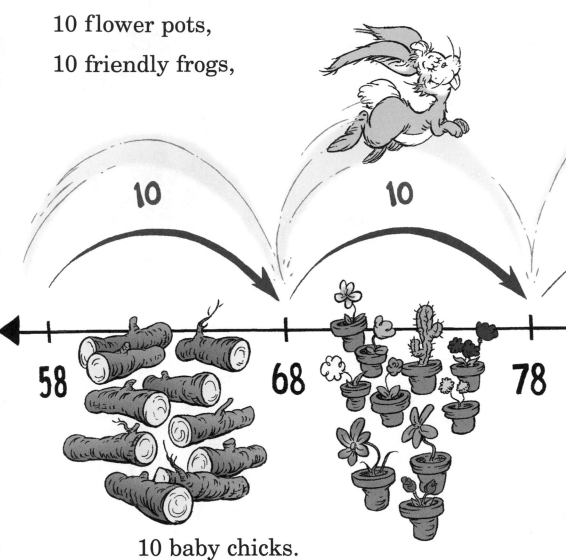

10 baby chicks.

(She's getting tired, it's true.)

Next she'll hop over turtles,

but there are just 2.

58+42=100

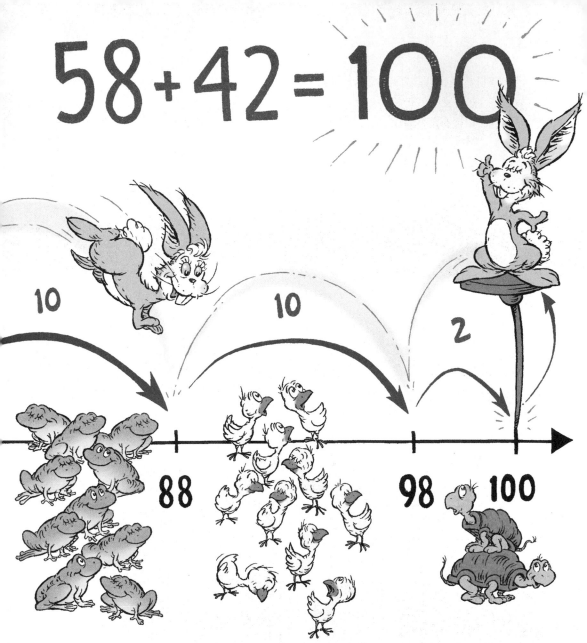

10   10   2

88   98   100

Hippity did it!

And now you can see

58 and 42

add up to 100! Yippee!

Next is a story
by Thing One and Thing Two
about 100 bees.
I will read it to you.

One day 100 bees
flew off into the sky
away from their hive.
(We have no idea why!)

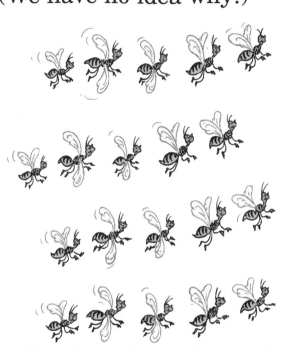

The first thing they did
(we both thought this was nifty)
was fly through the air in
2 big groups of 50.

When they got farther
away from the hive,
they flew in 4 smaller groups . . .

They were flying so far
that a small bee named Jack
said, "It's getting late and
I want to go back!"

The bees turned around
to go back home, and then
this time they flew in . . .

. . . 10 groups of 10.

"There it is!" said the biggest bee.

"I see the hive!

Now let's fly in . . .

"We made it!" yelled Jack.
"I think flying is fun,
but I'd just like to say that
I'm glad we are DONE!"

The End

29

FIELD TRIP TO FARMER FINKLE'S FARM!

Farmer Finkle has 100 hens.
They like living in groups
of 25 hens
and they live in 4 coops.

Her hens lay lots of eggs,
and the eggs that they lay
can sometimes add up to . . .

Farmer Finkle divides them
into 5 equal trays.
20 eggs in each tray
she will use different ways.

These eggs will help me.
I am going to show
something about numbers
that you might not know.

$100 \div 2 = 50$

50

There are odd and even numbers.
Even numbers, it's true,
can evenly be
divided by 2.

100 is an even number—
divide it by 2
and you will get 50
each time that you do.

What are odd numbers?
I'll give you a clue—
they *can't* be evenly
divided by 2.

99 ÷ 2 = 49
with **1** left over

99
is an odd
number.

49

99 is an odd number.

Divide it by 2—when you're done,

what is left over?

You see there is 1!

Today there's a party
for the Things' Grandpa Steven!
His family's a mix
of odd numbers and even.

It's his 100th birthday!
His family likes to play
tug-of-war, and they do it
in their own special way.

Even numbers on one side
and odd on the other.
(Thing One's on the opposite
side from his brother!)

Then comes the cake—
100 candles on top!
Grandpa will need help
when he blows them all out!

Now we're back in class
(I think this is cool).
The celebration continues—
what a great day of school!

I'm so proud of you,
and as I always say,
"You're 100 days smarter
than you were the first day!"

Count up YOUR school days.
When will your 100th day be?
Whenever it is,
you can party with me!

GLOSSARY

Add: To put together two or more numbers to get a single number. For example, when you put 2 and 3 together, you get 5.

Chart: A diagram or table that shows specific information.

Divide: To separate into two or more equal parts.

Multiply: To add a number to itself a specific number of times.

Opposite: On the other side or across from another person or thing.

Skip: To jump or leap over.

Skip count: To count (add or subtract) by a number other than 1.

Subtract: To take away from.

Sum: The number that results from adding two or more numbers together.

Total: The whole amount.

FOR FURTHER READING

Do Not Open This Math Book: Addition + Subtraction by Danica McKellar, illustrated by Maranda Maberry (Crown). Children and parents will want to OPEN this math book that bridges the gap between old-school and new-school math! For grades 1 and up.

How Much Is a Million? by David M. Schwartz, illustrated by Steven Kellogg (Lothrop, Lee & Shepard). In this classic award-winner, a clever math magician helps children understand the meaning of the number one million. An ALA-ALSC Notable and a *Horn Book* Fanfare Honor. For preschool and up.

Missing Math: A Number Mystery by Loreen Leedy (Two Lions). When math "goes missing" all around town, the problems are countless! From missing time to useless money, nothing gets done without numbers. For preschool and up.

Place Value by David A. Adler, illustrated by Edward Miller (Holiday House). Math is seriously delicious business for these baker monkeys. Uses easy and humorous visuals to help readers remember that 2 and 200 are not the same. For preschool and up.

Ten Black Dots by Donald Crews (Greenwillow Books). This unique graphic picture book shows how ten is more than just a number! For preschool and up.

INDEX

The Cat in the Hat's Learning Library®